CODE: STEM

SPACE TECH

Real-world coding projects made fun

Max Wainewright

WAYLAND
waylandbooks.co.uk

First published in Great Britain in 2019
by Wayland

Text copyright © ICT Apps, 2019
Art and design copyright © Hodder and
Stoughton, 2019

Credits:
Editor: Elise Short
Designer: Matt Lilly
Cover Design: Peter Scoulding
Illustrations: John Haslam

Every attempt has been made to clear copyright.
Should there be any inadvertent omission please
apply to the publisher for rectification.

HB ISBN: 978 1 5263 0879 5
PB ISBN: 978 1 5263 0880 1

Printed and bound in China

FSC
www.fsc.org

MIX
Paper from
responsible sources
FSC® C104740

Picture credits:
NASA on the Commons 6, 26, Shutterstock: Wangkun Jia 9, 12,
Space Faction/Getty Images, based on NASA material 10,
Shutterstock: Sunny studio 18, Shutterstock: 3Dsculptor 22.

Wayland
An imprint of
Hachette Children's Group
Part of Hodder and Stoughton
Carmelite House
50 Victoria Embankment
London EC4Y 0DZ

An Hachette UK Company
www.hachette.co.uk
www.hachettechildrens.co.uk

We recommend that children are supervised at all times when using the internet.
Some of the projects in this series use a computer webcam or microphone. Please
make sure children are made aware that they should only allow a computer to access
the webcam or microphone on specific websites that a trusted adult has told them to
use. We do not recommend children use websites or microphones on any other
websites other than those mentioned in this book.

Contents

Introduction 4

Project: Blast Off! 6

Project: In Control 10

Project: Gravity 15

Project: Jetpack 18

Project: Jetpack Game 21

Project: Satellites 22

Project: Return to Earth 26

Bugs and Debugging 30

Glossary.................................... 31

Index 32

Introduction

In this book we will look at some key concepts used in space technology, and explore them through coding. We will find out about gravity and how to overcome it to travel through space.

We'll be creating code to simulate how rockets and spaceships move. In order to experiment with the effects of gravity, we will store the value of gravity in a variable. By using a variable to model gravity, we will be able to make gravity more or less strong to see what effects it has on Earth, on the Moon or even on other planets.

You'll use the algorithms and ideas in this book, (and your imagination!), to travel through space, creating your own programs. These programs will help you understand how space technology works, and set you on the path to dreaming up your own ideas to voyage through the universe.

There are lots of different ways to create code.
We will be using a website called Scratch to do our coding.

Type **scratch.mit.edu** into your web browser, then click Create to start a new project.

Let's start by looking at the important parts of the screen in Scratch:

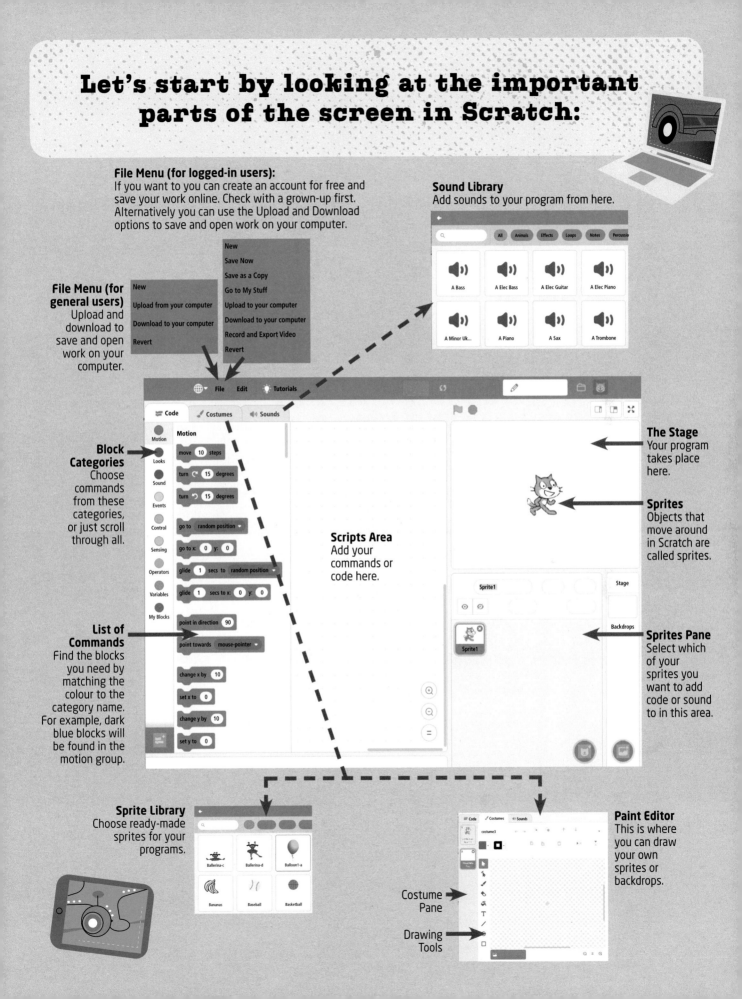

File Menu (for logged-in users):
If you want to you can create an account for free and save your work online. Check with a grown-up first. Alternatively you can use the Upload and Download options to save and open work on your computer.

File Menu (for general users)
Upload and download to save and open work on your computer.

New
Upload from your computer
Download to your computer
Revert

New
Save Now
Save as a Copy
Go to My Stuff
Upload to your computer
Download to your computer
Record and Export Video
Revert

Sound Library
Add sounds to your program from here.

All Animals Effects Loops Notes Percussio

A Bass   A Elec Bass   A Elec Guitar   A Elec Piano
A Minor Uk...   A Piano   A Sax   A Trombone

Block Categories
Choose commands from these categories, or just scroll through all.

List of Commands
Find the blocks you need by matching the colour to the category name. For example, dark blue blocks will be found in the motion group.

Code   Costumes   Sounds

Motion
Looks
Sound
Events
Control
Sensing
Operators
Variables
My Blocks

Motion
move 10 steps
turn 15 degrees
turn 15 degrees
go to random position
go to x: 0 y: 0
glide 1 secs to random position
glide 1 secs to x: 0 y: 0
point in direction 90
point towards mouse-pointer
change x by 10
set x to 0
change y by 10
set y to 0

Scripts Area
Add your commands or code here.

The Stage
Your program takes place here.

Sprites
Objects that move around in Scratch are called sprites.

Sprite1
Stage
Backdrops

Sprite1

Sprites Pane
Select which of your sprites you want to add code or sound to in this area.

Sprite Library
Choose ready-made sprites for your programs.

Ballerina-c   Ballerina-d   Balloon1-a
Bananas   Baseball   Basketball

Code   Costumes   Sounds
costume3

Paint Editor
This is where you can draw your own sprites or backdrops.

Costume Pane

Drawing Tools

Blast Off!

Let's start by launching a rocket into space. We'll create a simple countdown, then make our rocket move up, up and away.

Real rockets have to overcome gravity to take off. They do this by using very powerful engines that produce a massive amount of thrust.

Our program will simulate both of these forces by using a coding concept called a variable.

You'll find out more about gravity and thrust later on in this book.

STEP 1 - Remove the cat

Space is no place for a cat, so Right-click on the cat, then click **delete**.

STEP 2 - The backdrop

Click the **Backdrops** tab.

For help go to:
www.maxw.com

STEP 3 - The sky

Click **Convert to Bitmap**.

Choose light blue.

Select the **Fill** tool.

Click in the Drawing Area to draw the sky.

Click the undo tool if you make a mistake.

STEP 4 - The ground

Choose dark green.

Select the **Rectangle** tool.

Filled   Outlined

Set the rectangle to **Filled**.

Drag the mouse to draw the ground.

STEP 5 - Add a sprite

Click the **Choose a Sprite** button.

STEP 6 - Add a rocket

Rocketship

Scroll through to find the **Rocketship**. Click on it.

STEP 7 - How much power?

The rocket will start off with no power coming from its engines. We will then gradually increase the power until the rocket takes off. To be able to change the amount of power, we will store it in a variable. As we are dealing with rocket power, we will call the variable thrust.

Type **thrust**.

New variable

New variable name:

thrust

For all sprites   For this sprite only

More Options

Cancel   OK

Click the **Code** tab.

Operators

Variables

Click the **Variables** category.

Make a Variable

Click **Make a Variable.**

Click **OK**.

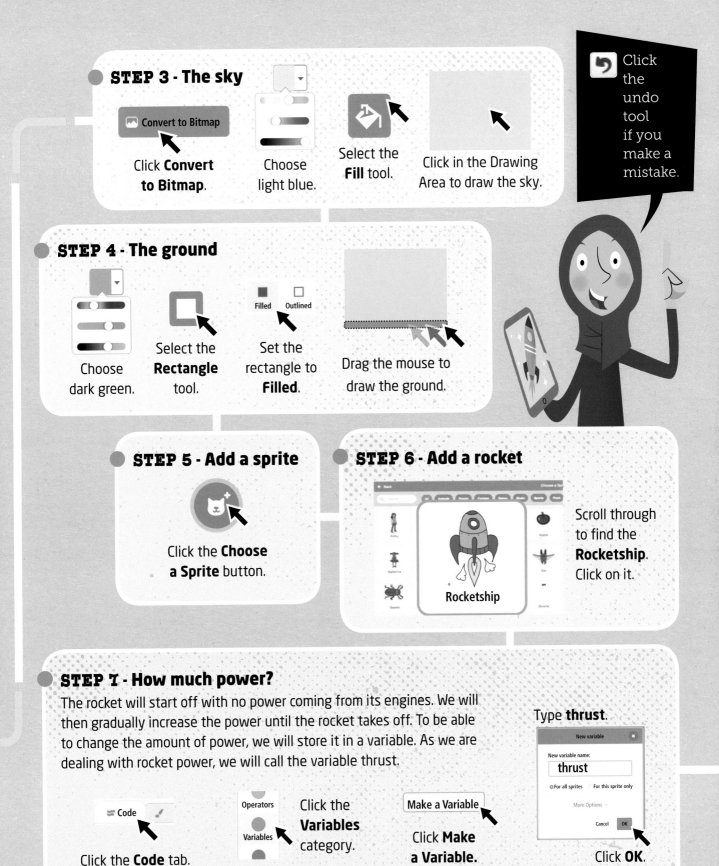

STEP 8 - Gravity

Everything on Earth is subject to a force called gravity. Gravity pulls the rocket to Earth and hinders it from taking off. To simulate this in our program we will create a variable called **gravity**.

Operators

Variables

Click the **Variables** category.

Make a Variable

Click **Make a Variable.**

Type **gravity**.

New variable

New variable name:
gravity

○ For all sprites   For this sprite only

More Options ▸

Cancel   OK

Click **OK**.

The gravity on Earth is 9.8 m/s² (metres per second squared). On other planets and their moons the value of gravity is different.

STEP 9 - The code

Drag the following code into the Scripts area.

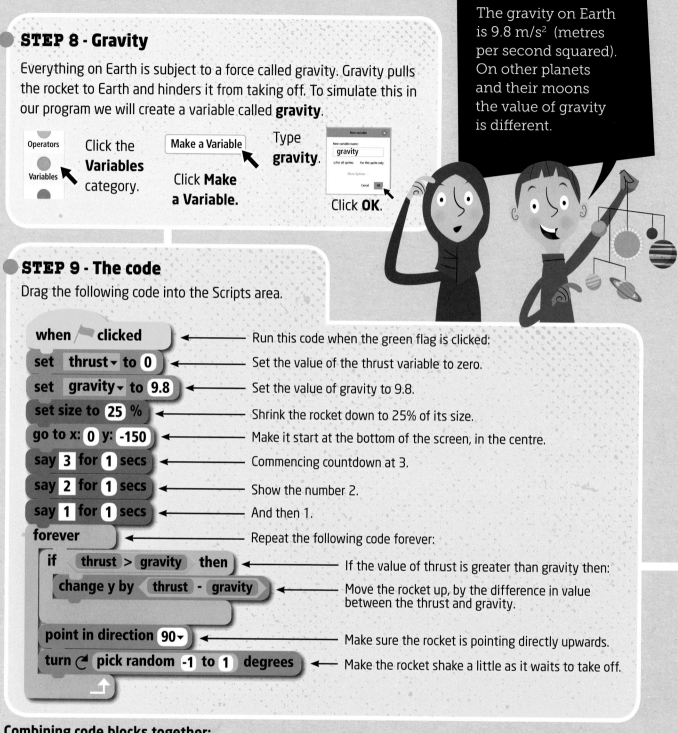

when ⚑ clicked ← Run this code when the green flag is clicked:

set thrust ▾ to 0 ← Set the value of the thrust variable to zero.

set gravity ▾ to 9.8 ← Set the value of gravity to 9.8.

set size to 25 % ← Shrink the rocket down to 25% of its size.

go to x: 0 y: -150 ← Make it start at the bottom of the screen, in the centre.

say 3 for 1 secs ← Commencing countdown at 3.

say 2 for 1 secs ← Show the number 2.

say 1 for 1 secs ← And then 1.

forever ← Repeat the following code forever:

if thrust > gravity then ← If the value of thrust is greater than gravity then:

change y by thrust - gravity ← Move the rocket up, by the difference in value between the thrust and gravity.

point in direction 90 ▾ ← Make sure the rocket is pointing directly upwards.

turn ↻ pick random -1 to 1 degrees ← Make the rocket shake a little as it waits to take off.

Combining code blocks together:

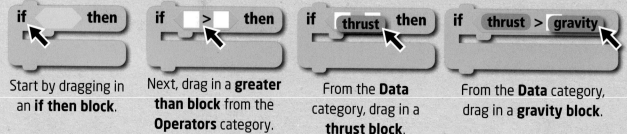

if ⬚ then

Start by dragging in an **if then block**.

if ⬚ > ⬚ then

Next, drag in a **greater than block** from the **Operators** category.

if thrust then

From the **Data** category, drag in a **thrust block**.

if thrust > gravity

From the **Data** category, drag in a **gravity block**.

8

STEP 10 - More thrust

We need to be able to increase the thrust so that the rocket takes off.
Drag in another section of code to do this:

```
when space ▾ key pressed
change thrust by 1
```

Run this code every time the space bar is pressed:

Increase the thrust by one.

⚑ **Now click the green flag to test your code.**

Each time you press the space bar the thrust value will increase. When it gets to ten the rocket will slowly start to rise. Keep pressing it to make it accelerate.

How it works — the rocket

Launching a rocket is a bit like letting air out of a balloon. As the air escapes out of a balloon one way, it pushes the balloon in the opposite direction. A rocket works in the same way, but instead of air, it blows out hot exhaust gases.

As the exhaust gases come out of the end of the rocket, they cause an equal and opposite reaction that pushes the rocket upwards.

A rocket has to carry fuel and a source of oxygen so it can burn even if there is no air, as is the case in space.

Code challenge

Make the countdown start from 5. Add a message that says 'blast off' before it takes off.

Change the code to make your rocket accelerate more quickly when the space bar is pressed.

Add some code to make the rocket take off automatically.

Why not try to draw your own rocket? Click on the rocket sprite then choose the Costumes tab. Click on the 'Paint new costume' icon and start designing your own rocket!

In Control

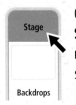

Now we've escaped from Earth's gravity and we're in space! But how do we control a spaceship or rocket once it's left Earth? The rocket's main engines will keep us moving forwards, but how about steering or changing course?

We will need some smaller thrusters fixed to the side of the spaceship in addition to the large main rocket engine. These allow us to change direction. Let's make our own spaceship to try this out.

STEP 1 - Seeing stars

We need to show a dark background with nothing but stars.

 Click on the **Stage** icon next to the sprites pane.

 Choose the **Backdrops** tab.

 Click the **Choose a Backdrop** icon.

Stars

Click on **Stars**.

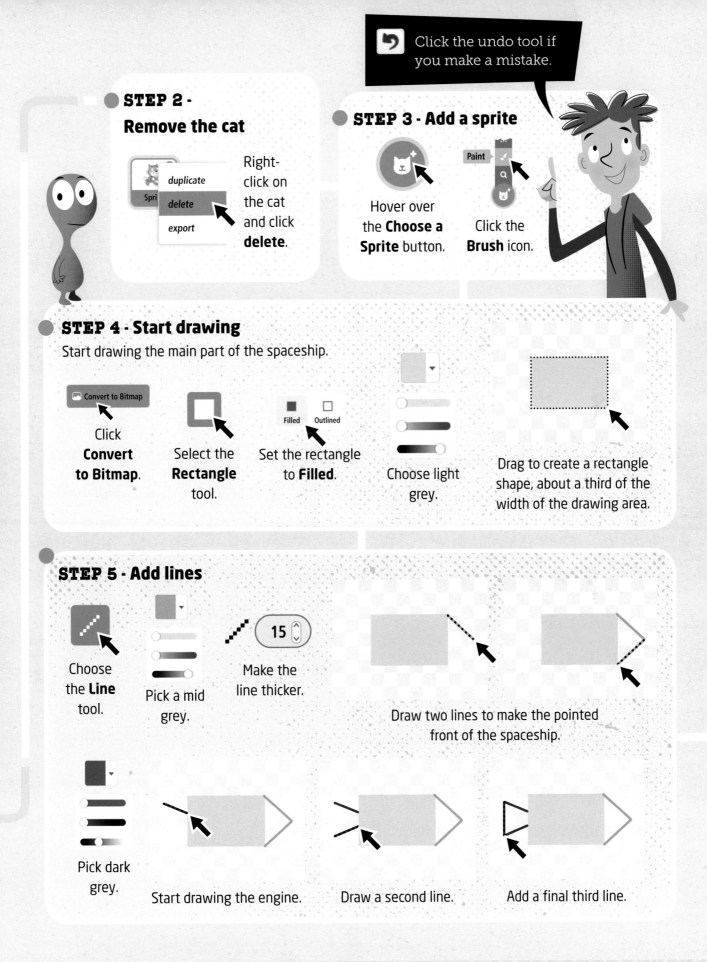

Click the undo tool if you make a mistake.

STEP 2 - Remove the cat

duplicate
delete
export

Right-click on the cat and click **delete**.

STEP 3 - Add a sprite

Paint

Hover over the **Choose a Sprite** button.

Click the **Brush** icon.

STEP 4 - Start drawing

Start drawing the main part of the spaceship.

Convert to Bitmap

Click **Convert to Bitmap**.

Select the **Rectangle** tool.

Filled   Outlined

Set the rectangle to **Filled**.

Choose light grey.

Drag to create a rectangle shape, about a third of the width of the drawing area.

STEP 5 - Add lines

Choose the **Line** tool.

Pick a mid grey.

15

Make the line thicker.

Draw two lines to make the pointed front of the spaceship.

Pick dark grey.

Start drawing the engine.

Draw a second line.

Add a final third line.

STEP 6 - Fill in

Choose the **Fill** tool.

Fill the engine with colour.

Select the mid grey again.

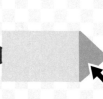
Fill in the front of the spaceship.

How it works
The Reaction Control System

One way to control the direction of a spaceship is to add some small additional engines called thrusters. These are like tiny rockets, one hundred times less powerful than the main engine.

The Reaction Control System (RCS) on this Apollo module is made from groups of four thrusters fixed to different parts of the spaceship.

Firing one of the thrusters on the left of the spaceship pushes the spaceship to the right. Firing a thruster on the right pushes it to the left.

STEP 7 - Add a Reaction Control System

The RCS needs to be quite small. Use the zoom controls to make it easier to see what you are drawing.

Select the **Brush** tool. Choose dark grey and make the line thicker.

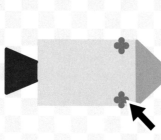

Draw a group of four thrusters on each side of the spaceship to create your RCS.

To see the main engine and RCS firing, let's add some simple animation to our program. To do this, we need to create three more pictures of the spaceship by duplicating the 'costume' – the picture of the spaceship.

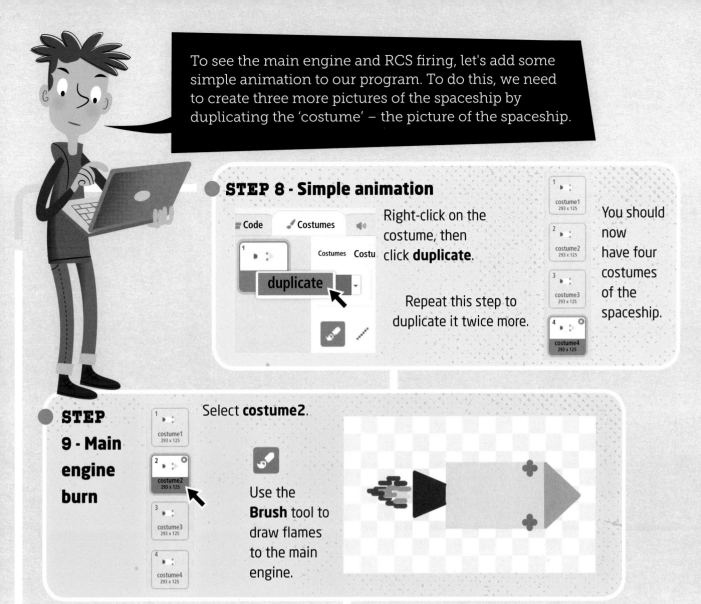

STEP 8 - Simple animation

Right-click on the costume, then click **duplicate**.

Repeat this step to duplicate it twice more.

You should now have four costumes of the spaceship.

STEP 9 - Main engine burn

Select **costume2**.

Use the **Brush** tool to draw flames to the main engine.

STEP 10 - Left and right

Select **costume3**.

Draw small flames coming from one side of the thruster group.

Select **costume4**.

Now draw small flames coming from the thruster group on the other side of the spaceship.

STEP 11 - Speed

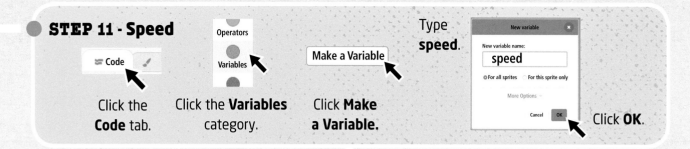

Click the **Code** tab.

Click the **Variables** category.

Click **Make a Variable.**

Type **speed**.

Click **OK**.

STEP 12 - The code

Drag the following code into the Scripts Area.

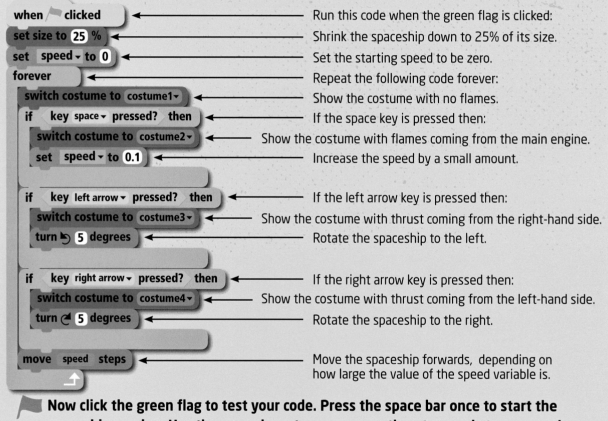

when ⚑ clicked — Run this code when the green flag is clicked:

set size to 25 % — Shrink the spaceship down to 25% of its size.

set speed ▾ to 0 — Set the starting speed to be zero.

forever — Repeat the following code forever:

switch costume to costume1 ▾ — Show the costume with no flames.

if key space ▾ pressed? then — If the space key is pressed then:

switch costume to costume2 ▾ — Show the costume with flames coming from the main engine.

set speed ▾ to 0.1 — Increase the speed by a small amount.

if key left arrow ▾ pressed? then — If the left arrow key is pressed then:

switch costume to costume3 ▾ — Show the costume with thrust coming from the right-hand side.

turn ↺ 5 degrees — Rotate the spaceship to the left.

if key right arrow ▾ pressed? then — If the right arrow key is pressed then:

switch costume to costume4 ▾ — Show the costume with thrust coming from the left-hand side.

turn ↻ 5 degrees — Rotate the spaceship to the right.

move speed steps — Move the spaceship forwards, depending on how large the value of the speed variable is.

⚑ **Now click the green flag to test your code. Press the space bar once to start the spaceship moving. Use the arrow keys to power your thrusters and steer around.**

Code challenge

Make the spaceship accelerate more rapidly when the space key is pressed.

Make the spaceship turn more slowly when the left and right keys are pressed.

Make the spaceship bounce off the edge of the screen when it reaches it.

Add an extra set of thrusters to the RCS and an extra costume. Make the spaceship slow down when the 's' key is pressed.

Gravity

Let's have a more detailed look at the force called gravity. Gravity attracts all objects towards each other. However the effect of this force is only truly felt when one of the objects is massive. Earth's gravity is strong because it is much bigger than any other object nearby.

Objects on Earth are pulled towards its centre by gravity. Other planets and the Moon also exert gravity. We're going to start by making a simple program that simulates how gravity works on Earth.

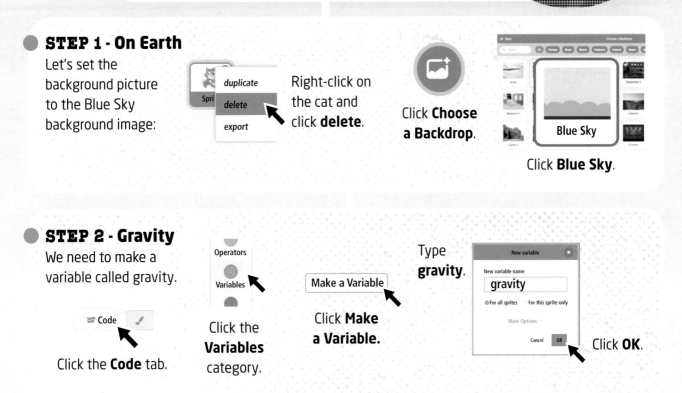

STEP 1 - On Earth

Let's set the background picture to the Blue Sky background image:

duplicate
delete
export

Right-click on the cat and click **delete**.

Click **Choose a Backdrop**.

Blue Sky

Click **Blue Sky**.

STEP 2 - Gravity

We need to make a variable called gravity.

Operators
Variables

≈ Code

Click the **Code** tab.

Click the **Variables** category.

Make a Variable

Click **Make a Variable.**

Type **gravity**.

New variable

New variable name:

gravity

For all sprites   For this sprite only

More Options

Cancel   OK

Click **OK**.

STEP 3 - Speed

Gravity pulls falling objects towards the centre of the Earth. This makes falling objects accelerate. To simulate this in our program we need to make a variable called speed.

Operators

Variables

Click the **Variables** category.

Make a Variable

Click **Make a Variable.**

Type **speed**.

New variable

New variable name:

speed

For all sprites   For this sprite only

More Options

Cancel   OK

Click **OK**.

STEP 4 - Add a sprite

Hover over the **Choose a Sprite** button.

Paint

Click the **Brush** icon.

STEP 5 - Draw a stick person

We need to draw a simple stick person. Start by drawing a head.

Select the **Circle** tool.

Filled   Outlined

Set it to **Filled**.

Pick **black**.

Drag to create a circle.

The stick person needs to be about three-quarters of the height of the drawing area. We'll shrink it with code later on.

STEP 6 - Arms and legs

Select the line tool.

40

Make the line thicker.

Use the line tool to add a body, arms and legs.

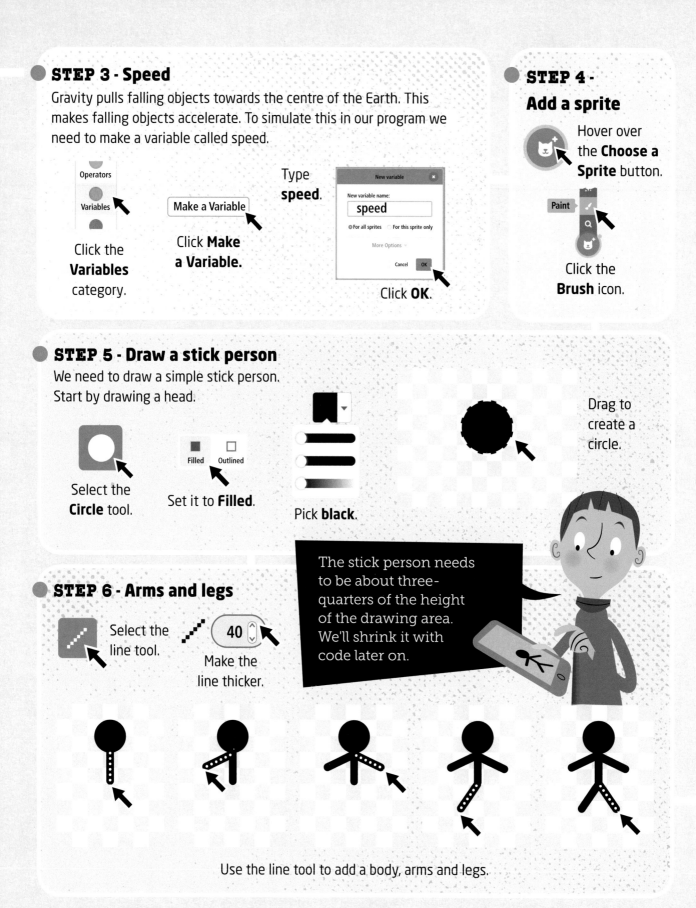

Now let's create code to make our stick person subject to the force of gravity, and see what happens!

STEP 7 - The code

Code

Click the **Code** tab, then drag the following code into the **Scripts Area**.

when 🏴 **clicked** ← Run this code when the green flag is clicked:

set size to 20 % ← Shrink the stick person down to 20% of their size.

set gravity ▾ to -9.8 ← Set the value of gravity to -9.8 (making it -9.8 will make sure it moves downwards).

set speed ▾ to 0 ← Start with the stick person not moving.

go to x: 0 y: 150 ← Position the person at the top of the screen, in the middle.

repeat until touching colour ● ? ← Keep repeating the following code until it reaches the ground.

  change speed ▾ by gravity / 50 ← Change the speed because of the force of gravity acting on the person.

  change y by speed ← Change the y value of the stick person according to its speed.

🏴 **Now click the green flag to test your code.**

Setting the colour

touching colour ●

Start by clicking inside the square.

Below the colour sliders, click on the **Pipette** tool.

Now click on the colour you need on the Stage.

Investigate

Change the starting position for the stick person by editing the 'go to x and y' values. What happens? Do they take longer to fall to Earth? Do they hit the ground as quickly?

We used -9.8 as our value for gravity. What happens if you use 9.8?

For help with combining the code blocks together, see page 8.

Code challenge

Create a second person to test gravity by duplicating the stick person. (Right-click on the sprite, then choose duplicate.) Change the starting position for the new stick person by editing the x and y values in the 'go to' code block.

y

Remember the x value tells Scratch how far across the stage a sprite is positioned, and the y value tells it how far up the stage.

x

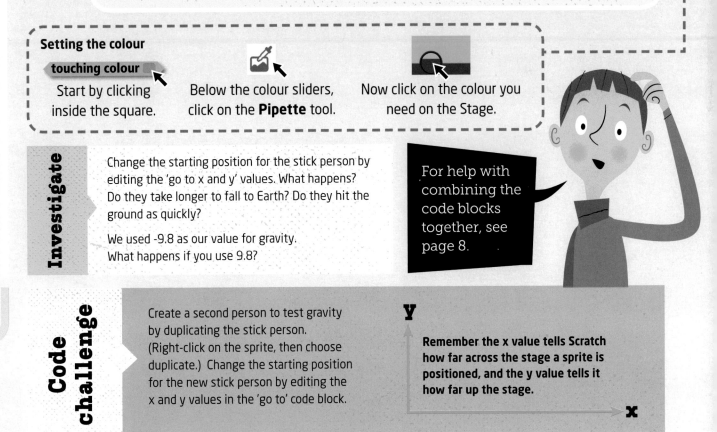

Jetpack

For help go to:
www.**maxw**.com

People have dreamed of escaping from Earth's gravity for thousands of years. Science fiction writers have dreamed up various flying devices.

One of the most exciting is the 'jetpack' – a pair of miniature rockets strapped to the wearer's back. In recent times real working jetpacks have been built. They've been used in space, on land and even at sea. We don't recommend you try and build your own jetpack – but we can try and create one with code.

STEP 1 - Before you start
Make sure you have all the code from the previous three pages in your computer and that the gravity is making your stick person fall down the screen.

STEP 2 - Change the sprite

✏ Costumes

Click the **Costumes** tab.

STEP 3 - Add a Jetpack
Draw a simple jetpack on top of the stick person.

Select the **Rectangle** tool and set to **Filled**.

Pick dark grey.

Draw three rectangles to make the jetpack.

STEP 4 - Add final details

Draw a jumpsuit for the stick person.

Select the **Line** tool.

Choose a colour.

Draw five lines to make the clothes.

Add any final details.

STEP 5 - Duplicate

Code | Costumes

duplicate

costu... 180 x 251

Right-click on the costume, then click **duplicate**.

Repeat this step to duplicate it again.

1 Costume1 180 x 251

2 Costume2 180 x 251

3 Costume3 180 x 251

You should now have three copies of the costume.

STEP 6 - Left and right

1 Costume1 180 x 251

2 Costume2 180 x 251

3 Costume3 180 x 251

Choose **costume2**.

Use the **Brush** tool to draw flames coming from the **left** side of the jet pack.

1 Costume1 180 x 251

2 Costume2 180 x 251

3 Costume3 180 x 251

Now select **costume3**.

Next, draw flames coming from the **right** side of the jet pack.

STEP 7 - Left key

Code

Click the **Code** tab then drag the following code into the Scripts Area.

Run this when the left arrow key is pressed:

Show the flames from one side.

Tilt it.

Increase its speed upwards.

```
when left arrow ▾ key pressed
switch costume to costume2 ▾
turn ↻ 2 degrees
change speed ▾ by 2
```

STEP 8 - Right key

Drag in this code for the right key:

```
when right arrow ▾ key pressed
switch costume to costume3 ▾
turn ↺ 2 degrees
change speed ▾ by 2
```

STEP 9 - Main code

Edit the original code from the gravity program so it looks like this. (The first five blocks are the same. You can drag the rest of the original blocks back to the block palette.)

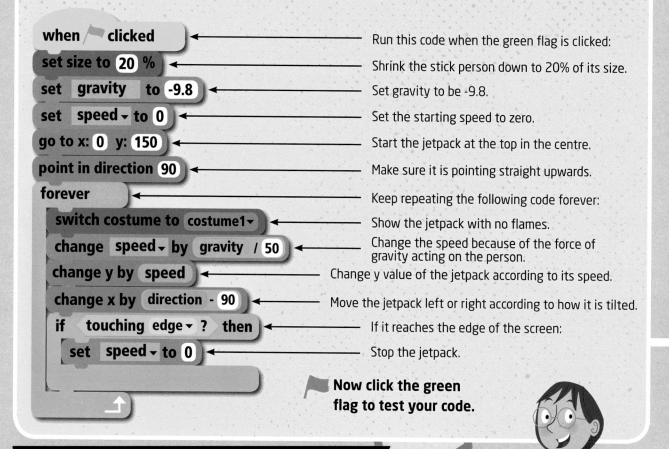

when ⚑ clicked	Run this code when the green flag is clicked:
set size to 20 %	Shrink the stick person down to 20% of its size.
set gravity to -9.8	Set gravity to be -9.8.
set speed ▾ to 0	Set the starting speed to zero.
go to x: 0 y: 150	Start the jetpack at the top in the centre.
point in direction 90	Make sure it is pointing straight upwards.
forever	Keep repeating the following code forever:
switch costume to costume1▾	Show the jetpack with no flames.
change speed ▾ by gravity / 50	Change the speed because of the force of gravity acting on the person.
change y by speed	Change y value of the jetpack according to its speed.
change x by direction - 90	Move the jetpack left or right according to how it is tilted.
if touching edge ▾ ? then	If it reaches the edge of the screen:
set speed ▾ to 0	Stop the jetpack.

⚑ **Now click the green flag to test your code.**

Press the left and right cursor keys quickly on the keyboard to fire the jetpack, and keep it balanced! Practise flying around the screen.

Code Challenge

Let's change our program to simulate being on the Moon...

Start by changing the backdrop to a more suitable one, like the Moon or space:

The gravity on the Moon is 1.6 m/s². Work out how to change your code to set the value of gravity to -1.6 . You will need delicate fingers to control your jetpack in this low-gravity environment!

Find out the value of gravity on other planets and test your jetpack across the universe.

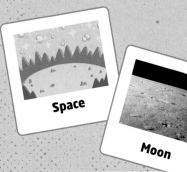

Space

Moon

Jetpack Game

Before you start make sure you have a working jetpack and all the code from the last couple of pages!

We can turn the jetpack program into a simple game. The aim of the game is to collect as many rocks as possible in one minute.

STEP 10 - The score

We need to make a variable to store the score:

Make a Variable

Go to the **Variables** category and click **Make a Variable.**

New variable

New variable name:

score

○ For all sprites ○ For this sprite only

More Options

Cancel   OK

Type **score**.

Click **OK**.

STEP 11 - Add a sprite

Click the **Choose a Sprite** button.

Rocks

Scroll through to find the **Rocks** sprite and click on it.

STEP 12 - Rock code

⇌ Code

Click the **Code** tab, then drag the following code into the **Scripts Area**.

```
when 🏳 clicked
set size to 25 %
reset timer
set score ▾ to 0
repeat until   timer > 60
    set x to  pick random -160 to 160
    set y to  pick random -80 to -160
    wait until   touching Sprite1 ▾ ?
    change score ▾ by 1
    play sound pop ▾

say Time up!
```

Run this code when the green flag is clicked:

Shrink the rock down to 25% of its size.

Set the timer back to zero.

Set the score back to zero.

Repeat the following code for one minute:

Position the rock in a random position across the screen.

But make sure it is near the bottom.

Wait until the rock is touched by the jetpack (Sprite1).

Increase the score by one.

Play a sound effect.

Show a message at the end.

🏳 **Test your code.**

21

Satellites

A satellite is something that orbits a planet. The Moon is a natural satellite. There are also thousands of artificial satellites in orbit around Earth.

Satellites are used for all sorts of purposes including communication and navigation. SATNAV devices, for example, use satellites to work out where we are. They are also used to study space and Earth, and to predict the weather.

STEP 1 - Stars

Let's start by picking a dark background with nothing but stars.

Right-click on the cat, then click **delete**.

Click on the **Stage** icon next to the sprites pane.

Click the **Choose a Backdrop** icon.

Stars

Click on **Stars**.

Normally, moving objects want to keep moving in a straight line (this is called momentum). But the force of gravity also pulls a satellite back towards Earth. When the two forces of momentum and gravity are balanced, the satellite travels around the Earth in a curved path called an orbit.

STEP 2 - The Earth

Earth

Click the **Choose a Sprite** button.

Scroll through to find **Earth** and click on it.

STEP 3 - Rotate

Click the **Code** tab, then drag this code into the Scripts Area.

when 🏳 clicked

go to x: 0 y: 0

forever

    turn ↻ 1 degrees

Run this code when the green flag is clicked:

Position the Earth in the centre of the screen.

Keep repeating this code forever:

Rotate the Earth very slowly.

STEP 4 - Add a satellite

Hover over the **Choose a Sprite** button.

Click the **Brush** icon.

Most satellites use solar panels to provide their power. The panels are quite large and look like wings. (But remember, as they are in orbit they don't need wings!)

STEP 5 - Start drawing

Draw the solar panels of the satellite first. They should be about half the height of the drawing area.

Click **Convert to Bitmap**.

Select the **Rectangle** tool.

Set the rectangle to **Filled**.

Choose pale blue.

Drag to create the panels.

Choose grey, then draw the body of the satellite.

Choose the **Line** tool. Change to dark grey.

Draw lines to add detail to the solar panels.

Click the undo tool if you make a mistake.

23

STEP 6 - Speed variable

Create a variable to store the speed of the satellite.

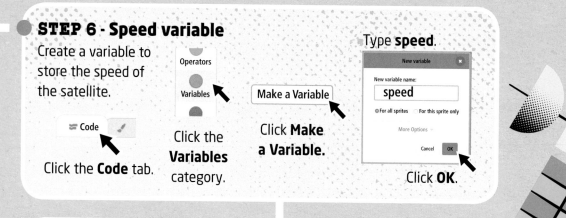

Operators

Variables

Click the **Variables** category.

Make a Variable

Click **Make a Variable.**

Type **speed**.

New variable

New variable name:

speed

● For all sprites   ○ For this sprite only

More Options >

Cancel   OK

Click **OK**.

≈ Code

Click the **Code** tab.

STEP 7 - The code

Drag this code into the Scripts area to make the satellite orbit the Earth.

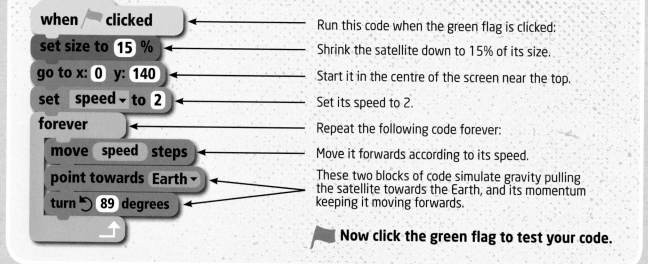

when ⚑ clicked

set size to **15** %

go to x: **0** y: **140**

set **speed ▾** to **2**

forever

move **speed** steps

point towards **Earth ▾**

turn ↻ **89** degrees

Run this code when the green flag is clicked:

Shrink the satellite down to 15% of its size.

Start it in the centre of the screen near the top.

Set its speed to 2.

Repeat the following code forever:

Move it forwards according to its speed.

These two blocks of code simulate gravity pulling the satellite towards the Earth, and its momentum keeping it moving forwards.

⚑ **Now click the green flag to test your code.**

The Earth should slowly rotate, and the satellite should orbit around it. (Because we aren't using 3D images the Earth will spin rather than rotate the way it really does).

Now we will turn our satellite into a communications satellite. It will simulate sending messages down to Earth and back.

STEP 8 - Add another sprite

Click the **Choose a Sprite** button.

Ball

Scroll through to find **Ball** and click on it.

STEP 9 - Communication code

This code will simulate a radio signal being transmitted back and forth between the Earth and the satellite. Drag it into the Scripts area.

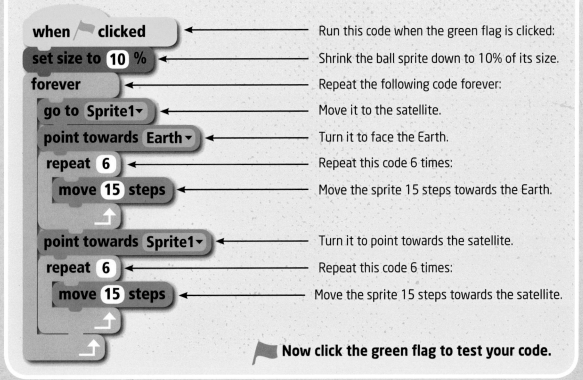

when ⚑ clicked	Run this code when the green flag is clicked:
set size to 10 %	Shrink the ball sprite down to 10% of its size.
forever	Repeat the following code forever:
go to Sprite1▾	Move it to the satellite.
point towards Earth▾	Turn it to face the Earth.
repeat 6	Repeat this code 6 times:
move 15 steps	Move the sprite 15 steps towards the Earth.
point towards Sprite1▾	Turn it to point towards the satellite.
repeat 6	Repeat this code 6 times:
move 15 steps	Move the sprite 15 steps towards the satellite.

🚩 **Now click the green flag to test your code.**

Investigate

Try changing the value in the set size code blocks. What happens?

Change the amount turned in the turn right code block for the satellite. Try using 80 instead of 89 degrees. What happens? Try using a larger number.

Code challenge

Try changing the value of the satellite's speed variable from 2 to a slightly smaller or larger value. Can you make the satellite stay over one part of the Earth and rotate at the same speed as the Earth? This is called a geostationary satellite.

Create a second satellite by duplicating. Change its code to make sure it starts in a different place.

Return to Earth

Rockets and spaceships are usually built from separate modules or parts.

Only small parts of a spaceship return to Earth. The Apollo missons used parachutes to slow down the Command Module on its return to Earth, and splashdown into the ocean. Let's recreate this with code.

STEP 1 - The sea and sky

Let's start by drawing the sky and the sea.

Right-click on the cat, then click **delete**.

Choose the **Backdrops** tab.

STEP 2 - Start drawing

Start with the sea.

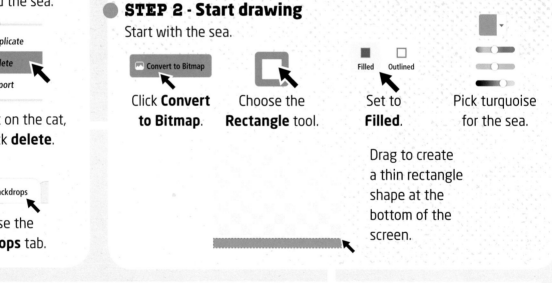

Click **Convert to Bitmap**.

Choose the **Rectangle** tool.

Set to **Filled**.

Pick turquoise for the sea.

Drag to create a thin rectangle shape at the bottom of the screen.

STEP 3 - Blending colours

We need to create a sky that is black at the edge of space, fading through to blue below.

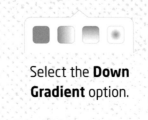

Select the **Fill** tool.

Choose black.

Select the **Down Gradient** option.

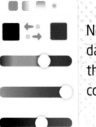

Now pick dark blue as the second colour.

Click the undo tool if you make a mistake.

STEP 4 - The sky

Click to colour in the sky.

STEP 5 - Add a sprite

Hover over the **Choose a Sprite** button.

Paint

Click the **Brush** icon.

STEP 6 - Draw the Command Module

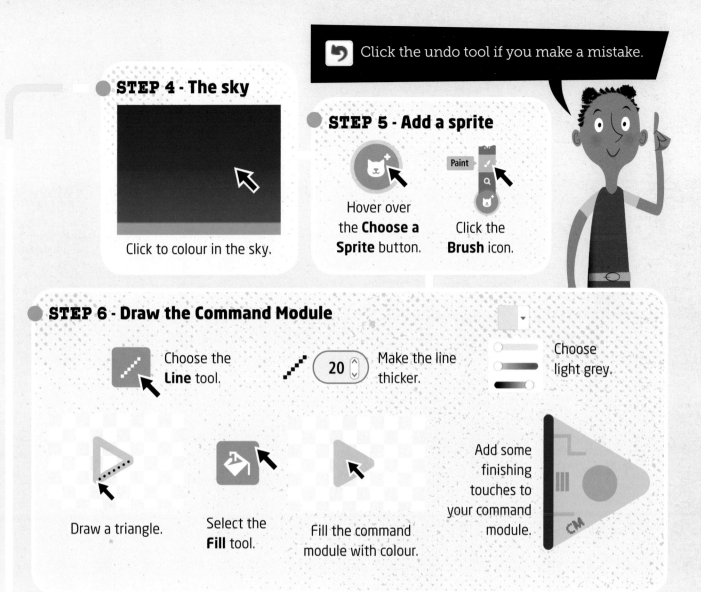

Choose the **Line** tool.

Make the line thicker. **20**

Choose light grey.

Draw a triangle.

Select the **Fill** tool.

Fill the command module with colour.

Add some finishing touches to your command module.

CM

STEP 7 - Duplicate

We need to draw a second version of the spaceship, with a parachute. Remember, Scratch calls this second picture a costume.

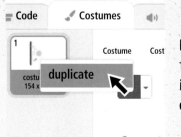

Code Costumes

Costume Cost

1
costu
154 x

duplicate

Right-click on the costume icon, then click **duplicate**.

1

Costume1
154 x 204

2

Costume2
154 x 204

A copy of the costume should appear.

III

CM

Once our returning command module gets close to Earth, gravity will start to make it fall very quickly. We will need to add a parachute to reduce the effect of gravity and allow it to land more slowly.

STEP 8 - Draw the Parachute

Select the **Circle** tool.

Set it to **Filled**.

Filled   Outlined

Select red.

Carefully draw a large oval above the spaceship.

Choose the **Select** tool.

Drag a selection box around half of the oval.

Press the delete key (backspace on a Mac) to remove the left half.

STEP 9 - Attach it

Choose the **Line** tool.

Pick dark grey.

7

Make the line thicker.

Draw some ropes to connect the parachute.

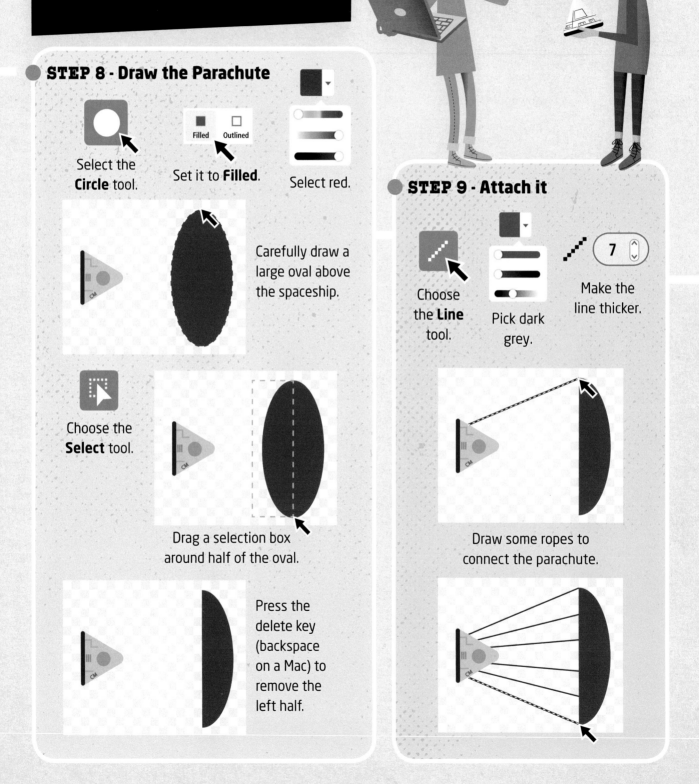

STEP 10 - Rock code

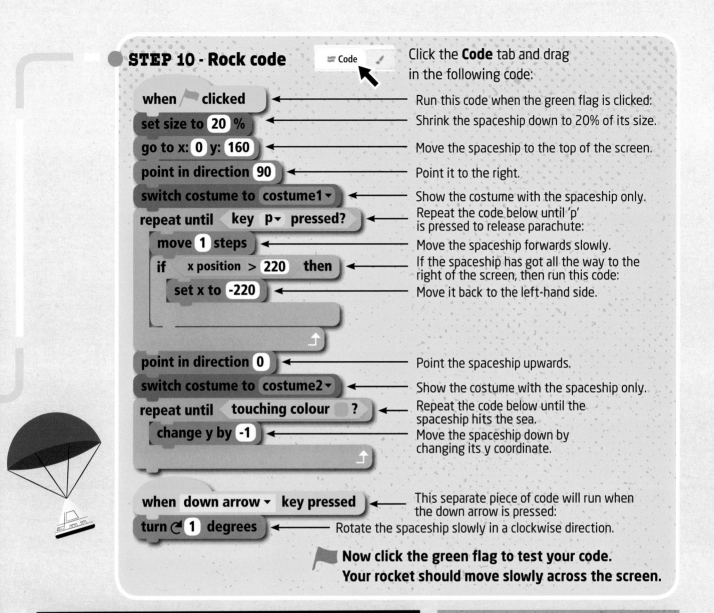

Code ✎

Click the **Code** tab and drag in the following code:

when 🚩 **clicked** ← Run this code when the green flag is clicked:

set size to `20` **%** ← Shrink the spaceship down to 20% of its size.

go to x: `0` **y:** `160` ← Move the spaceship to the top of the screen.

point in direction `90` ← Point it to the right.

switch costume to `costume1 ▾` ← Show the costume with the spaceship only.

repeat until `key p ▾ pressed?` ← Repeat the code below until 'p' is pressed to release parachute:

　move `1` **steps** ← Move the spaceship forwards slowly.

　if `x position > 220` **then** ← If the spaceship has got all the way to the right of the screen, then run this code:

　　set x to `-220` ← Move it back to the left-hand side.

point in direction `0` ← Point the spaceship upwards.

switch costume to `costume2 ▾` ← Show the costume with the spaceship only.

repeat until `touching colour ▨ ?` ← Repeat the code below until the spaceship hits the sea.

　change y by `-1` ← Move the spaceship down by changing its y coordinate.

when `down arrow ▾` **key pressed** ← This separate piece of code will run when the down arrow is pressed:

turn ↻ `1` **degrees** ← Rotate the spaceship slowly in a clockwise direction.

🚩 **Now click the green flag to test your code.**
Your rocket should move slowly across the screen.

Press the down arrow to slowly aim the spaceship towards the sea. When the spaceship is low enough, press the 'p' key to release the parachute. It should then gently glide down to the sea.

Code challenge

The parachute should slow the spaceship down considerably. Change the code to make it fall even more slowly.

If the spaceship enters the atmosphere at too steep an angle it will get hot and could burn up. Add some code that checks to see if the angle is more than 105 degrees and gives a warning message. It should also stop the program.

Investigate

What happens if you change the 220 and -220 values in the 'if' code block? What are the best values for your spaceship to use?

Bugs and debugging

If you find your code isn't working as expected, stop and look through each command you selected. Think about what you want it to do, and what it is really telling the computer to do. If you are creating one of the programs in this book, check that you have not missed a line. Some things to check:

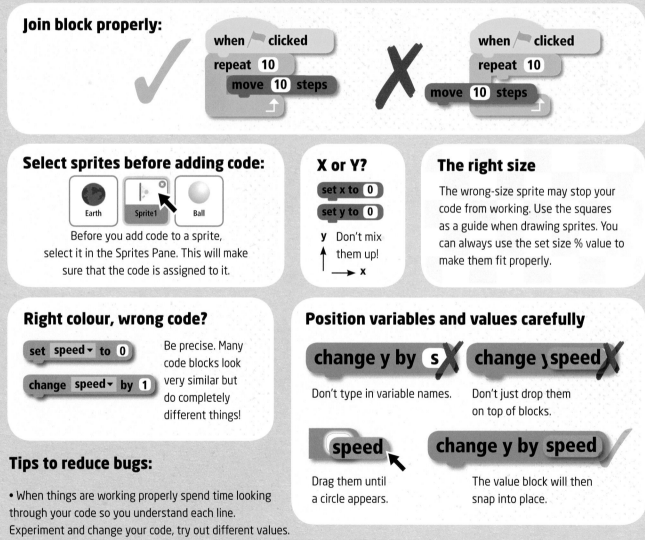

Join block properly:

when ⚑ clicked
repeat 10
    move 10 steps ✓

when ⚑ clicked
repeat 10
move 10 steps ✗

Select sprites before adding code:

Earth Sprite1 Ball

Before you add code to a sprite, select it in the Sprites Pane. This will make sure that the code is assigned to it.

X or Y?

set x to 0
set y to 0

y Don't mix
↑ them up!
→ x

The right size

The wrong-size sprite may stop your code from working. Use the squares as a guide when drawing sprites. You can always use the set size % value to make them fit properly.

Right colour, wrong code?

set speed ▾ to 0

change speed ▾ by 1

Be precise. Many code blocks look very similar but do completely different things!

Position variables and values carefully

change y by s ✗   change y speed ✗

Don't type in variable names.   Don't just drop them on top of blocks.

speed

Drag them until a circle appears.

change y by speed ✓

The value block will then snap into place.

Tips to reduce bugs:

• When things are working properly spend time looking through your code so you understand each line. Experiment and change your code, try out different values. To be good at debugging you need to understand what each code block does and how your code works.

• Practise debugging! Create a very short program and get a friend to change just one block while you aren't looking. Can you fix it?

• If you are making your own program, spend time drawing a diagram and planning it before you start.

• Try changing values if things don't work, and don't be afraid to start again – you will learn from it.

Glossary

Algorithm – rules or steps followed to make something work or complete a task.

Bug – an error in a program that stops it working properly.

Code block – a draggable instruction icon used in Scratch.

Conditional – a block of code that only runs if something is true.

Debug – removing bugs (or errors) from a program.

Degrees – the units used to measure angles.

Gravity – a force that pulls objects together.
   It is only noticeable if one of the objects is massive, e.g. a planet.

Icon – a small clickable image on a computer.

Jetpack – a complex low-powered rocket system worn on your back.

Loop – repeating one or more commands a number of times.

Orbit – the circular path taken by one object around another (usually) bigger one.

Parachute – a device that slows down a falling object by using air resistance.

Random – a number that can't be predicted.

RCS – (Reaction Control System) a group of thrusters working together to steer a spaceship.

Right-click – clicking the right mouse button on a sprite or icon.

Satellite – an object (e.g. a moon or a communications device)
   that orbits around another object, such as a planet.

Sequence – commands that are run one after another in order.

Sprite – an object with a picture on it that moves around the stage.

Stage – the place in Scratch that sprites move around on.

Steps – small movements made by sprites.

Thrust – the force that pushes something along, e.g. a rocket's engines.

Variable – a value used to store information in a program that can change.

Index

A
animation 13

B
backdrops 5-6, 10, 15, 20, 22, 26
bugs 30

C
colour, adding 7, 11-12, 16, 18-19, 23, 26-28
command blocks 5, 8-9, 14, 17, 19-21, 23-25, 29-30
co-ordinates (x, y) 8, 17, 20-21, 23-24, 29-30
costumes 9, 13-14, 18-20, 27

D
debugging 30
drawing 5, 7, 9, 11-13, 16, 18-19, 23, 26-28

G
gravity 4, 6, 8, 10, 15-20, 22, 24, 28

J
jetpack game 21
jetpacks 18-20

M
momentum 22, 24

P
parachutes 26-29

R
Reaction Control System 12-14
rocket, launching a 4, 6-9

S
satellites 22-25
sprite, adding a 5, 7, 9, 11, 16, 21-24, 27, 30

T
thrust 6-9
thrusters 10-14

V
variables 4, 6-8, 14-16, 21, 24-25, 30

FURTHER INFORMATION

Gifford, Clive. *Get Ahead in Computing* series. Wayland, London, UK: 2017.

Wood, Kevin. *Project Code* series. Franklin Watts, London, UK: 2017

Wainewright, Max. *Generation Code: I'm an Advanced Scratch Coder.* Wayland, London, UK: 2017.